SELF-MASTERY

&

ENLIGHTENMENT

THROUGH THE

KINGDOM OF PLANTS

Forge a Connection With Nature, Understand Your Role in the Ecosystem, Draw Inspiration From Plants, and Cultivate a Positive Mindset in Serving Them

by

Dr. MANOJ SARKAR

Dr. ARUNA BASU

Email: manojkumarsarkar1954@gmail.com

Author website: https://niveditatrichy.org

ACKNOWLEDGEMENTS

My humble gratitude to **Mr. Som Bathla,** who is an Amazon #1 **Bestselling author** of multiple books; for mentoring, motivating, and guiding me to **Write, Self-Publish, & Launch Books** and for helping me start my Authorpreneur Journey.

I am thankful to Mr. Ravi Tewari and Mr. Sooraj Achar, who are also Amazon's #1 **Bestselling authors** of multiple books, for their **help** in publishing this book.

Did you know live in a kingdom? This isn't one created by humanity arguing over scepters and silken robes, though - this is the Kingdom of Plants or the 'kingdom Plantae,' which includes all flora, from miniscule mosses to massive trees. Plants merit this regal title. As research in the Proceedings of the National Academy of Sciences USA finds, with over 4.00,000 known species, they account for 80% of the total biomass or life forms on Earth. Bacteria come second at a distant 15% - humans are 0.01%.

- Craig Brodersen, Times Evoke; TOI, Chennai June 24,2023

Why worry if tigers and rhinos and a few plant species are wiped out? An environment in which animals and plants became extinct is not safe for human beings either?"

- Indira Gandhi

The Kingdom of Plants or Kingdom Plantae humanity 80% of the food we eat and 98% of the oxygen we inhale.

The extraordinary Kingdom of Plants is now under siege. The State of the World's Plants and Fungi Report finds that 40 % of these species face different degrees of threats including even their extinction.

- Craig Brodersen, Times Evoke; TOI, Chennai June 24, 2023

WHY IS THIS BOOK FOR YOU?

1.   For our daily needs, we heavily depend on the generous services from the Kingdom of Plants, which includes all flora, from miniscule mosses to massive trees. They provide us 80% of the food we eat and 98% of the O2 we inhale. You can survive for some days without food, but can you stay even a minute in the absence of O2? Plants produce O2 for all living beings. We have become a cog of the machine and forgotten the roots of our survival. This book enlightens you about all the facts through the Kingdom of plants; seek your love and care for them.

2.   The plant kingdom works as a storehouse to supply all the basic life-supporting systems (BLISS! e.g., food, air, water, fertile soil, life-saving drugs, etc.). Besides tangible and intangible benefits flow, the Plant Kingdom also extends blessings through its subtle voice and communicates wisdom to the aspirants through their spirit of unending services in silence as monks. I experienced this communication and benefitted in many ways. Your true love and positive mindset in serving them can connect you to them... It can bring miracles and fulfillment to your life. This book shares the experience with you.

3.   You get an opportunity to meet a British man in India as an IFS Officer by the name Hugo wood who never wanted his

name, fame, money, or the result of his action but gave his everything to bring back the lost glory of greeneries of in Western Ghats, fighting against the then British Government even at his supreme sacrifice on 12.12.1933. I am sure this article on Hugo Wood (10th article) would inspire you to protect, conserve, and augment forests- the root cause of our survival.

TABLE OF CONTENTS

INTRODUCTION

Kingdom Plantae, or the Plant Kingdom, is the only living entity that sacrifices everything for the benefit of others, including mankind. The Forests in Sea and on land - the home of the Plant kingdom works as a store house to supply all the Basic Life Supporting System (BLISS!). Besides tangible and intangible benefits flow, the Plant Kingdom also extends subtle blessings and wisdom to the aspirants through their spirit of unending services in silence as monks. Thus, forests, as a composition of innumerable plants, operate as the 'Sea of Monks', being a panacea to human beings and other living organisms. These very facts urge for a committed, logical, and scientific approach to conserving, managing, and expanding our forest resources for the present as well as for the generations to come.

I acknowledge the source of everything that is in this book and accept my indebtedness to that infinite source of strength that exists in all living beings, especially in the form of kingdom plantae, which pulled me affectionately and instilled all wisdom documented in this book through their selfless service in silence.

Writing this book was not purely my wish but something that happened in a sequence of events. In 1986, I joined the Indian Forest Service after leaving my job as a Civil Hydrographic Officer in the Indian Navy. Forests and forestry were not familiar to me. It appeared to be a boon to me from an invisible source that destined me to join this service, do unselfish work, and enjoy the journey. However, in the first instance, I could not pass the Botany examination during the foundation course of this service at Indira Gandhi National Forest Academy, Dehra Dun, in 1987. This failure proved to be a blessing in disguise. I developed an unlikely hobby of 'Seed collection' of known and unknown flora and learned them intimately to pass this formal examination based on my newly acquired knowledge in the field of botany. This hobby later emboldened me to write articles on uncommon and lesser-known plants in dailies to create awareness among people about the invaluable services of the Kingdom of Plants or 'Kingdom Plantae.'

Finally, it gave me the experience of getting a vibrant connection with the Kingdom plantae after a gap of 18 years in the green campus of the Indian Institute of Management, Bangalore, in 2002. I was intuitively attached to plants and used to make solutions of classroom exercises of management school through plant-related issues while undergoing the PGPPM course on public policy at IIM, Bangalore (Post Graduate Programme in Public Policy and Management course for selected civil servants based on merit from all over the country for a year). There was one occasion when all the course participants were asked to submit combined papers (by a group of two but not more than three) on 'Ethics in public life.' Most of my colleagues proposed papers on corruption and ethics in public life, while I proposed ethics, if any, related to the indiscriminate destruction of plant life by human beings. The entire class thundered with laughter and made jokes. I smiled as I knew the subject through subtle communication from plants. Later on, our group (Dr Janaki Ananthakrishnan and I) scored the highest marks with the same concept.

The Hidden Voice of Plants of the Kingdom Plantae can be listened to by those who are fortunate to have a very deep understanding and who had the opportunity to serve them for a long time in protecting, conserving, and propagating them with true Love and Humility. WE HAD THE OPPORTUNITY. The whole story of this book entails the true experiences earned soon after joining the forest service and continues till today. It is part of our life.

The young seedlings of Gurjan, Dipterocarpus turbinatus ready to serve Mother Earth

Vedanta lays down three criteria of Truth:

i)   *Testimony of scripture that serves as a working hypothesis:*

ii)   Positive reasoning that seeks to separate the truly essential from the nonessential, and

iii) Personal experience.

All three must point to the same conclusion in order to establish the validity of the seeker's realization of Truth.

My personal experiences with members of kingdom plantae happened several times to realize the Truth that is narrated hereafter.

PART I: LOVE CONNECTS YOU TO THE KINGDOM OF PLANTS

1. MY EXPERIENCES WITH MEMBERS OF KINGDOM PLANTAE

1. My first interactions with the Kingdom of Plants:

This happened at IGNFA Campus, Dehra Dun, in 1987 when I could not pass in Botany (the subject which enables all about learning of the scientific fields of plant community, their names, characters, utility their society, and many other things without which one cannot go ahead about their relationship with the other species of animal kingdom particularly with special reference human beings). However, this failure appears to be a boon in disguise and made a Turning point in my life. The auspicious experience of this boon in disguise is reflected in the first article of this book.

2. My second meeting with a member of this community:

This meeting was very surprising and, through an unexpected positive indication, happened at IIM, Calcutta, at JOKA during the early morning of 1992. There was a compulsory Training Programme being conducted by the IIM, Calcutta, approved by the Min. of Forests and Environment, Govt. of India for a week. I was one of the trainees among other participants in the same service. Staying, with all other essential facilities, be provided by the authorities.

I maintained my usual daily routine of walking in the early morning to get the opportunity to see the sterling red color of the bright rising sun. Truly speaking, I used to be a greedy man in this regard, and I hardly missed any opportunity of this kind. Meeting the rising SUN in the early morning, one can get direct blessings from Him - a source of good health for all living on Mother Earth. Today, too, I was blessed and enjoyed humming the stotra of **"Pratasmarami of the Adi Shankaracharya"** while moving ahead. Visibility was normal, as it happens on winter mornings.

Suddenly, it happened to me, as if somebody called me 'Take my photograph.' I was all alone. I looked back and then left and right but could find none. I checked my mobile and found no symptoms of any sound. So, I took my forward steps, and again, I heard the clear voice, "TAKE MY PHOTOGRAPH." I dared to go back and looked down both sides of the path and observed a few groves of beautiful TOUCH ME NOT plants with blossoms of light pinkish-white color flowers. I sat there slowly for a while and cared for the beautiful flowers and leaves, touching them with the care of my love. As if they smiled at me, I, too, showed them my humble affection.

It was all in *ANUBHAV*, i.e., in deep experience within. It gave me a flush of joy and great satisfaction to observe the entire happening. I took a few photos of the small plant groves with my mobile phone and moved forward. I could get no more calls from the back! I was awake with full consciousness all through, and it was not an imagination.

Touch me not plant called me 'Take my photograph' at IIM Calcutta, Joka

3. My third Experience at IIM, Bangalore Camus, in 2002:

I joined there in a public policy course along with another 25 AIS and Central Services officers in the PGPPM course for a year. The selection of the candidates for the course was through tough competition amongst the AIS Officers and officers of Central Services from All India basis. I could make it at the age of 48 years. First, a few days with introductory classes was fine for me. After about 2 weeks, I found it was a really difficult course for me to continue here. Meanwhile, out of 28 officers who got selected, two officers left after attending classes for 2 weeks (paying the penalty), keeping us 26 in number in the IIMB journey.

But for me, it was equally difficult to leave the course as I had to pay Rs 2 Lakhs from my own pocket as a penalty for leaving the course in between. Further, the Government of Tamil Nadu wouldn't pay for me as it already sanctioned my candidature to bear the entire course cost for everything, including a foreign trip to a university to study for 3 months!

So, without being perplexed, I took it as a challenge and planned a strategy to rejuvenate my confidence level to cope with the situation. The management provided a Duplex accommodation with all self-sustaining facilities to all 26 officers. I cut short all my extra-curricular activities except a few habits, like getting up early in the morning, after taking a bath and sitting for some time to connect with the supreme self. Then, sit to complete homework assigned for the day and go to the open field just before the Sunrise. After hovering all along the boundary of a field 3 to 4 times with some chanting, I used to pluck a few fresh flowers to offer to my deities. This became some sort of regular practice.

However, the pressure was augmented with daily classroom presentations, individually in groups, along with paper submissions. One day, when I was very thoughtful and anxious about my presentation in the afternoon in a group of two. I reduced the number of times I hovered around the field and started plucking flowers carefully without causing injuries to the plant. Suddenly, a miracle happened, as if that plant had transpired to me what was to be done for my presentation today. I stood for a few minutes there and touched the plants with humility, and my living communication with the plants continued every day. My presentation was appreciated as I presented what I learned from the plant in the K-11 classroom.

After that, I solved all my classroom presentation, paper submissions based on lessons learned from the plants in general. It continued the entire period of the management school.

My duplex was full of seeds, plants, related books, etc. Susanto Das (one of my colleagues from the same course) asked me one day, 'Dada, how do you solve your every classroom problem through plant-related issues?' His question was again reflected on the page:

'The Pioneers' – a small book published at IIMB by all my fellow colleagues of the Public Policy Course (2002-2003)

Hobby: Communicating with Plants.

The man who lives like a plant….. (or is it the other way around?) The last of a vanishing species of homo-sapiens who delights in shocking visitors to his home with collection of seeds, weeds and beads. Manoj takes morning walks humming bhajans and talking to plants…Has a fetish for dissertations on endangered species and shlokas before every presentation... the "dada..moni" of the batch , is ever joyful .

We were taken to Syracuse University, USA, as a part of the public policy course for about 3 months. My connection with the plant kingdom continued there, too, and empowered me to present a real story on *Threatened plants in the United States of America and in India - a comparison of their protection status with respect to the existing policies available in both countries.* My story on threatened plants was adjugated by the expert committee, which awarded me an A+ in my credit.

4. Learning the plants and their Taxonomical names at AYYALUR, Dindugul District, Tamil Nadu:

After completing 2 years Professional course at *Indira Gandhi National Forest Academy*, Dehradun, and a Foundation course at *Lal Bahadur Shastry Academy of Administration*, Mussoorie, I joined at Patiala in Punjab then, re-joined at Ayyalur after getting my cadre transferred from Punjab to Tamil Nadu. At Ayyalur, I joined as a Trainee Assistant Conservator of Forests in Dindugul Forest Division, Dindugul district, during the middle of 1989.

Somehow, I passed the Botany exam, thanks to the knowledge I acquired from the Botanical Garden of *Forest Research Institute*, Dehradun. However, I deeply understood the value of knowing the taxonomical part of the subject for any forest officer. So, I was looking for a chance to expand my knowledge of it. My field staff was composed of two Foresters, 4 forest guards, and four forest watchers. All were Tamil persons, so language was not a problem.

I made a strategy and called for a meeting of all the field staff in a staggered manner so that the protection of the forest is not affected. I explained to them that on the salary day, each of them could bring some leaves, flowers, and fruits, if available, a few plants, and they could put in old newspapers or old magazines (whatever they were using) writing the local name of the plants whatsoever plants they bring. At the end of the day, I shall consult various books I had with me to find out the botanical names of the plants they have given to me.

This process really helped me to learn the local names of the plants and also their scientific names. It was good learning for me and helped me in my entire career to write articles in daily Newspapers and scientific articles in various journals /magazines and, finally, while carrying out my Ph.D. work on endemic and threatened medicinal plants.

At the end of the 3 months of training there, surprisingly, one day, the Conservator of Forests of the Trichy Circle, Shri K. Viswanath IFS, along with the District Forest Officer, Dindugul, came to the rest house in the afternoon. I received them as per the protocol. After some time, the conservator of forests told me that he would like to have a round inside the forest rest house campus.

I took a small notebook and pen to note any points he referred to. While perambulating inside the campus, he asked a dozen of names of trees, shrubs, herbs, etc. With my humble voice, I could reply to the local names, their scientific names for all the plants he asked for. The DFO was a little nervous about whether I would be able to answer. The CF hand shook me with a comment that you got 100 out of 100 marks and added further comment that 'I have taken this kind of test for many Trainee ACF, but none received cent percent marks.' I felt Happy. The DFO and the CF left for Dindugul in the evening.

I conveyed my happy greetings to all my field staff for their help. Through this process, I acquired knowledge about the scientific names of all species of the locality and the surroundings. It helped in many ways.

Further, I started learning the characters of the plant, their flowering and fruiting periods, and making notes on them. It further made me closer to the plant's community day by day. I used to feel my mindfulness with the world of plants and enjoy their connection even today.

PART II: VOLITION IN SERVING PEOPLE

2. TURNING POINT OF MY LIFE FROM THE HOBBY OF SEED COLLECTION

On 2 June 1986, I joined the Indian Forest Service at IGNFA (Indira Gandhi National Forest Academy), Dehradun, after leaving my job as a Civil Hydrographic Officer in the Indian Navy. Forests and forestry were not familiar to me. I felt as if it was a boon to me. It appeared that an invisible source destined me to join this service to carry out unselfish work and enjoy the journey of life. However, in the first instance, I could not pass the Botany examination during the professional course training of this Service at IGNFA, Dehradun, in 1987.

My revered mother smilingly told me, **"Love the plants to know them and grow them."** I could not understand the secret of this statement until I failed in Botany and finally passed it at IGNFA, Dehra Dun. It was a stunning lesson for me, and it is still stunning today.

To pass in botany during my IFS Training, I used to go to the local botanical garden on holidays at the FRI campus. I started learning the names of plants from the name board fixed on tree trunks. To know their names intimately, I started a collection of seeds from the nearby ground of the plant to memorize their difficult names. I started learning the names of plants and finally passed in botany. However, the seed collection remains with me as my new hobby. **It appeared to me that my loving plants *within have made a turning point in my life.***

This failure proved to be a blessing in disguise. It gave me a sense of deep understanding that to render good services in forests and forestry, one must love to learn certain basic things like Forest types, their composition, species names and their assemblage, their characteristics, growth habits, and how they can be further propagated.

During our All-India tours in North, South, East, and West, I fully enjoyed my new hobby and collected more than 415 types of seeds, pods, and dry fruits of plant species. It gave me great learning about their local names, scientific names, their various characteristics, and growth habits. I started a small nursery in front of my room in the New Hostel and got scoldings from Shri Kazmi Sir (Sports Instructor). Somehow, I continued my business to confirm the habits of learning about plants and their growth.

Created a tiny self-made Nursery in front of my room S-52 in the new hostel, IGNFA

I continued my business to confirm the habits of learning about plants and their growth. Three tall plants of *Polyalthiya longifolia*, which were planted at the end of 1987 in front of my hostel room as a mark of my love, can still be noticed today. (Photographs attached)

I preserved the collected seed pods for a long period until ants, insects, and rats attacked these seeds. Later on, I used them as my teaching tool to the trainee foresters in Forest Training College, Vaigai, Theni district, Tamil Nadu, as its Principal and Chief Conservator of Forests from September 2009 to October 2010.

Meanwhile, Shri KVSK Reddy, IFS, one of my seniors and the Director of Arignar Zoological Park, Vandalur, Chennai, called me to provide some good colorful seeds /pods to the park for making an exhibit for awareness creation of the tourists who visit the park every day. I gladly gave him various kinds of seeds, which he displayed nicely for the tourists to learn (the photo below).

(Exhibits showing seeds/pods kept in AZP and me with Shri
KVSK Reddy, Director, AZP)

Finally, I kept the remaining seeds in plastic containers, arranged them sequentially in two wooden racks, and presented them to the Institute as training materials (vide: Photograph).

Collected seeds of various trees, shrubs, climbers, etc.,
were maintained in plastic containers and put in racks as
study material to train in-service forestry students at TNFTC,
Vaigai dam

I could collect the seeds, pods, bark, fruits, etc., during the All-India tours from the following areas:

A-Tour in part of the Himalayas (Himachal Pradesh and Jammu and Kashmir)

B- Tour in the Western part of India (Rajasthan, Gujarat)

C-Tour in part of Northern and Eastern India (Punjab, Haryana and Uttar Pradesh)

D-Tour in part of Southern India (Kerala and Tamil Nadu)

The hobby of collecting seeds gave me joy and insight as if the" seeds of love "were sown in me for the Kingdom Plantae for my lifetime. It gave me a living bond with the plant community.

This gave me the endeavor to put the best services for the plants in terms of their protection, conservation, and augmenting of them wherever I was posted. Besides, I was also taking up awareness creation about the goodness of plants or even protection problems of flora and fauna.

I continued my connection with plants in various ways more vigorously by growing them wherever I worked. Besides writing about them in scientific journals and daily newspapers, I wrote project reports and finally did my Ph.D. and wrote books on plants to create awareness and love for plants. My objective was to learn and share the learning with all so that love for plants grows among people as their committed care for plants helps in the protection of forests and also grows by planting them.

Three seedlings of *Polyalthiya longifolia* were raised in my small nursery from the collected seeds and planted in front of my hostel room at the end of 1987.

These three small seedlings were raised in my tiny nursery, and now they are grown up as tall trees as my own children, grown up as smart and able to support their father! Yes, they are my own. I Hug each of them! I wished them for their future safety. It gave me an enormous sense of joy when I visited them in November 2022 along with my batchmates, who attended two days of senior officers' meetings on the IGNFA and FRI campuses.

Three seedlings of *Polyalthiya longifolia* were raised in my tiny nursery in 1987, and now they are tall trees.

This hobby later emboldened me to write articles on lesser-known plants in dailies to create awareness among people about the invaluable services of the plant kingdom.)

Finally, it gave me the experience of getting a vibrant connection with the plant kingdom after a gap of 18 years in the green campus of the Indian Institute of Management, Bangalore, in 2002. I could solve all classroom exercises of management school through plant-related issues while undergoing the PGPPM course on public policy at IIM, Bangalore. (PGPPM-Post Graduate Programme in Public Policy and Management course for selected civil servants based on merit from all over the country). Intuitively, I felt as if the plant kingdom, for all such solutions, bestowed me direction and blessed me.

This inspired me to write a dissertation on dying and decaying plants (threatened plant species) in the country for the same course.

I remember the golden words of my mother even today.

3. "FORESTS" - A STOREHOUSE FOR SUPPLYING THE BASIC LIFE SUPPORTING SYSTEMS. 1397

Namely Air, Water, Fertile soil, and Life-Saving Drugs, etc. FOR ALL THE LIVING BEING ON THE EARTH".

KINGDOM OF PLANTS

We are in the Kingdom of Plants or 'Kingdom Plantae' that includes all flora, from miniscule mosses to massive trees. Our lives depend on plants - we must value their contributions, and we must acknowledge, appreciate, and take all measures to protect and propagate them for our own survival.

The research Proceedings of the National Academy of Sciences USA observes that with over 4,00,000 known species, they account for 80% of total biomass or lifeforms on Earth. Bacteria stand second with only 15%, whereas we humans cover 0.01%.

Land plants first appeared 500 million years ago on Earth, with trees emerging 370 million years ago. As the number of plants increased, they removed more and more carbon dioxide from the atmosphere, cooling the Earth and emitting oxygen, enabling mankind and other animals. It was the majestic science of plants - their photosynthesis turns water, sunlight, and carbon dioxide into oxygen and sugars—

that made human life possible through the gifts of air and food.

The Kingdom of Plants or Kingdom Plantae humanity 80% of the food we eat and 98% of the oxygen we inhale.

The extraordinary Kingdom of Plants is now under siege. The State of the World's Plants and Fungi Report finds that 40% of these species face different degrees of threats, including even their extinction. *The plant species are confronting the large-scale destruction of habitat for commercial farming, livestock rearing, and construction in the name of development. Plants are embattled by climate change, caused by anthropogenic emissions alerting the Earth's air, water, and heat, triggering floods, droughts, fire, and pestilence. The Food and Agriculture (FAO) finds that 40% of all crops are already lost annually, leaving millions facing hunger.*

(Craig Brodersen, Times Evoke)

For survival, man needs food to eat, air to breathe, water to drink, and life-saving drugs at the time of his ailments. All these requirements form the Basic Life Supporting System for human beings.

Forests work as a storehouse for supplying all these basic life-supporting systems to mankind, including other animals and microcreatures.

In the conventional system of valuation of forests, the benefit flow of tangible parameters was mainly calculated. All existing public policies are mostly limited within the benefit flows, mainly fuel, fodder, timber, etc., while the importance of Forests has to be evaluated more deeply for the posterity of all living beings. Hence, the existing policies, both at the state and national level, need to be looked into more carefully, especially in

- Policies related to the felling of trees.

- Total protection and conservation-oriented controlling system.

- An inventory to be carried out for all plant resources of all Districts / Forest Division (as a unit of the entire country).

- Soon after inventory, the biochemical test and quantity of various alkaloids, etc., are to be made to finalize the suitability of the plants.

- Special attention is to be paid to making an inventory of all plants that are on the verge of different degrees of threats, and comprehensive action is to be taken to ensure their identification, total protection, conservation, and propagation without further delay.

i) Medicinal Plants for Life-Saving Drugs:

After finding out the list of plants with Medicinal properties – the plants with life-saving drugs are to be separated.

Their Zone of Endemism maps can be prepared, and special care may be given to such plants both for their protection, conservation, and further propagation and for patenting such plants of rare availability for preparing life-saving drugs.

ii) Major Percentages of Gases Flow in the Atmosphere:

Gas	Symbol	Content in %
Nitrogen	N2	78.084%
Oxygen	O2	20.947%
Argon	Ar	0.934%
Carbon dioxide	CO2	0.035%

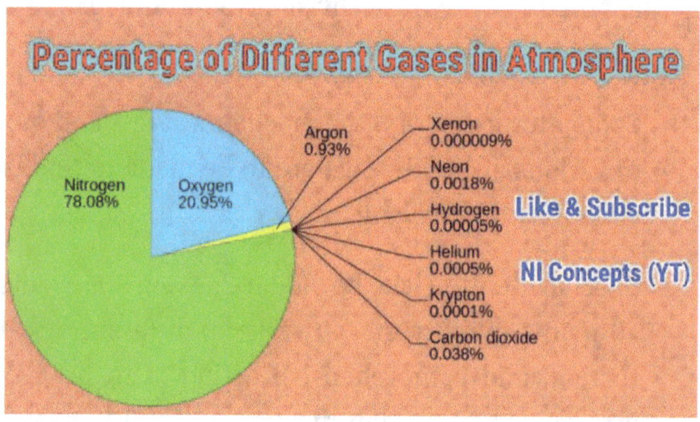

All of Earth's oxygen does not come from trees. Rather, the atmospheric oxygen that we depend on as humans comes predominantly from the ocean. According to National Geographic, about 70% of the oxygen in the atmosphere comes from marine plants and plant-like organisms.

These ocean-living plants release molecular oxygen as a waste product of photosynthesis (as do most plants). In photosynthesis, plants capture sunlight and use its energy to split carbon dioxide and water, making sugar for itself and releasing oxygen as a by-product.

The dominance of ocean life as Earth's top oxygen producer makes sense when you consider that the majority of the Earth is covered with ocean.

Of the different types of marine life providing oxygen, the dominant class is phytoplankton. Phytoplankton are microscopic photosynthesizing organisms that live in water. Phytoplankton includes cyanobacteria, green algae, diatoms, and dinoflagellates.

Although too small to be visible to the human eye by itself, when many phytoplankton clump together, they look like green ocean slime. The oxygen we depend on from breath to breath is provided mostly by a vast army of invisible sea creatures.

No more; it is a myth that there will not be any required O2 flow in the atmosphere if there is no plant on the Earth's surface. No plants – No creation of O2 in the atmosphere & hence, no breathing is possible for mankind & other animal kingdoms.

Plants - namely Trees, shrubs, herbs, grass, liana, climbers, etc., are the O2-producing factories. Forests, as the home of such trees, shrubs, Herbs, etc., are the gigantic O2-producing factories blessed by nature for the survival of human beings.

However, we, the less foresighted people – still claim, provoke, and recommend the diversion of forestlands for non-forestry purposes and tree felling – in the name of so-called development!

We all want development. Still, in India, more than 70% of people live in villages– where living with Gandhian thought is very much possible. The *'Ramrajya'* can not only supply the basic needs of a greater number of people for a longer period but also can provide them a peaceful co-existence, cheerful living with the fulfillment of life, and also keep the home ready for future generations.

Of late, without appreciating the benefit for more people for a longer period, we often opt for quick, shortcut methods in the name of so-called development. Therefore, we lose our healthy living Eco-system of our surroundings by destroying the entire Air, Water, and Soil-producing factories, i.e., the Forests. We must, and should, praise the naturally gifted forests and protect them with all humility and honor.

Virtually there should be a total ban on any kind of tree felling on any part of the Earth's surface, whether it is Forestland or on any private premises. More stringent kinds of policies need to be thought of, and also more awakening needs to be built up among the people, students, planners, etc. so that everyone starts growing plants of their own for the amount of O2 he/she consumes every day. It does not logically support that we consume a large quantity of a resource that we never produce, nor pay for the consumption of this, nor even think for its protection!

Hence, there must be some policies that every family must plant and protect a minimum number of O2-producing factories or plants, failing which they do not possess the right to intake O2 freely from the atmosphere. They must pay tax for this non-committal activity and for putting the burden of their living on others' shoulders.

iii) Water Supply:

We get water from rain, from the subsoil, or from the flowing water like rivers or lakes. Truly speaking, the basic source of freshwater is precipitation, either in the form of raindrops or snowfall.

India is a fortunate country to have sufficient rainfall for a span of 4 to 5 months from the southwest and northeast monsoons. Even in some places, the rainfall is more than 8 months. However, unfortunately, without a sufficient storage system, in-situ infiltration in the sub-soil usually cannot happen in our country. Hence, almost more than 80% of such rainwater reaches the Bay of Bengal / Arabian Sea as surface runoff immediately after the rainfall.

What a misery! When a country gets a rainfall of 5 months of fresh water – but reaches the sea within no time - while the large section of the people in the same land still do not get the mere drinking water to drink!

To stop this surface runoff, what we have to do is enhance the forest cover all over the country, irrespective of the legal status of the land. At least 33% of the land needs to be covered with trees, shrubs, and herbs with 3 to 4-tire forest canopy cover. This helps to disperse each raindrop into minute particles and allows it to percolate slowly in the subsoil, enhancing the groundwater discharge and stopping the surface off.

What we need is a permanent plant cover of 33% of each individual household, preferably with a three-tier system. In civil works, a vegetative barrier can also be formed to stop the surface runoff. Some large-scale dams, lakes, etc., can also be formed. Hence, existing policies need to be taken care of from this angle.

iv) Source of Fertile Soils:

For producing food crops, we need fertile, loamy soil, which is mainly a mixture of humus colloids that comes mainly from plants or largely from forests. Mechanical use of chemical fertilizers proved to be fatal and destroyed soil health. Hence, Healthy, fertile soil that is the product of the forest has direct role in public life in producing food crops – using natural and fertile soils. The application of chemical fertilizers needs to be reduced, and policy decisions need to be made.

Finally, Public Policy for the protection of existing forests and Forestland, increasing the forest cover of the country, essentially needs to be framed. Further, protecting the fragile ecosystem – restoring fresh O_2 flow, promoting perennial water flow – protecting the natural water bodies, enhancing groundwater discharge, raising the groundwater table, and ensuring sustained yield of life-saving drugs from the forest are required to be outlined in Public Policy.

Awareness Creation about plants and their goodness through a few articles in Daily National Newspapers

(I continued my connection with plants in various ways more vigorously by growing them wherever I worked. Besides writing about them in scientific journals in daily newspapers, I wrote project reports, and finally, I did a Ph.D. and wrote books on plants to create awareness about the goodness of plants to all. Some of the articles published in daily National newspapers like The Hind and The New Indian Express are presented here.

However, some of these articles were oversized and quite old. Hence, copies of these articles are not very easy to go through. Therefore, these articles were retyped and placed herein for the convenience of the learned readers as follows:)

4. THE WOODS ARE LOVELY

(THE HINDU YOUNG WORLD)

21 March is World Forestry Day. Geographically, this is the day when seasonal changes coincide with the Equinox. Forests, classified as commercial resources, need to be protected and preserved. It is the responsibility of every individual to ensure that trees are planted and forests are protected.

21 MARCH, World Forestry Day, was thought of at the European Conference of Agriculture in 1971 in Spain. Consequently, the Food and Agriculture Organisation (FAO) decided that it would be celebrated in every country. Geographically, this day is when seasonal changes coincide with the Equinox, the date when day and night are equal. The day is also when spring ends and summer begins. Physiologically, in the plant kingdom, this day coincides with a period of gradual increase in photo-period and the onset of active growth period of plant tissues despite the relatively dry season.

Indian civilization, at all social levels, has been impregnated with environmental consciousness, which can be traced back to the Vedic period onwards. We in India do not look upon our forests as mere sinks for toxic emissions. Forests mean much more to us, more as a community resource linked to society, the economy, and culture.

While the rich talk about the ozone layer, global warming, and forests as sinks for carbon emissions, communities around forests worry only about their day-to-day struggle for basic commodities like water, firewood, and a square meal. For a layman away from the forests, the term conservation seems to be complicated.

In India, forests are not a mere sink of toxic emissions. They are community resources linked to society, the economy, and culture.

After independence, forests, in addition to being classified as commercial resources, were a resource that could be preserved and protected. With the changes in society, forest administration started losing its effectiveness. Several rules and regulations were passed to overhaul forest policies, yet they were not so effective from the social point of view. The preservation and protection that people could require even today were based on their social beliefs and rituals.

The natural pockets of vegetation maintained and preserved for centuries in the name of a village deity were usually looked after by the local communities. But seldom touched for any kind of produce. There are many rare species, and they are called sacred groves.

Forest management requires the cooperation of the people. Despite several attempts to preserve our biodiversity by declaring forests as protected ones, is there an example like the sacred groves maintained for several years by the local people without any incentive or directions from any agencies?

Community plantation for fodder and fuel

The rapid depletion of forests is attributed to the rapid population growth, but there are policies, especially the National Forest Policy: 1952, which recommends tree planting. Though such schemes are successful, people's participation in the preservation and protection of natural forests was not stressed. In 1981, the idea was thought of in Tamil Nadu and implemented as a part of joint forest management. The concept is around the protection of forests with a mutual understanding between the forest department and the people living near these areas.

A further step was taken with a policy of people's participation in forest management, implemented in 'Arabari' in West Bengal. About 20 states have launched the scheme.

Catching them from young to love the plants

The concept of pure air, pollution checks, and acid rain does not bother the common man. Unless the individual is assured of logical returns, he will not be motivated to grow trees. It is here that the idea of tree crops comes in. The generous growth of Mesquite (*Prosopis juliflora*) trees in the dry parts of southern India has fulfilled the household demands of the poorest of the poor. In fact, the wood cut from the forests is sold to ensure the family's daily income.

Under the joint forest management scheme, the States have liberalized the system of forest produce by providing free collection and sale of such produce. The 1988 National Forest Policy emphasizes improving the production and marketing of forest produce. If appropriate measures are initiated for this purpose, the economic returns will be good.

According to a survey done by the Ministry of Environments and Forests, over 8,000 plant species are used as medicinal plants. The estimated market value of allopathic medicines derived from plants used in traditional remedies is over $43 billion annually. When an individual realizes the necessity of planting and protecting trees, he/she will require no further motivation.

5. GRASS THAT CAN FIGHT ALL ODDS (VETIVERIA ZIZANIOIDES) PUBLISHED IN THE NEW INDIAN EXPRESS

It has been estimated that soil loss in India due to erosion is about 12,000 million tonnes per annum. The loss of nitrogen-phosphorus-potassium **(NPK)** is more than the country's fertilizer output.

Vetiver grass could be used as an ideal plant in dryland farming to prevent soil erosion and carry out soil and moisture conservation works at a low cost. Commonly called Khas-Khas, it grows naturally in plains, lower hills, river banks, and marshy areas of Haryana, Punjab, Gujarat, Uttar Pradesh, Bihar, Assam, and also in southern states.

Botanically named Vetiveria zizanioides, it is a densely tufted, perennial grass but sterile outside its natural habitat. It has no rhizomes or stolons. It is propagated by root divisions or slips.

Vetiver's spongy root system binds the soil to a depth of up to 3 meters. By forming a dense underground curtain along the contour of the land, the roots prevent riling, gullying, and tunneling.

Tuft root of vetiver   **Vetiver extracted from nursery bed**

A vetiver hedge is key to the in-situ moisture conservation in a rain-fed farming system. It serves as a guideline for oil plowing and planting on the contour and, in times of heavy er rain and storms, prevents K largescale erosion. Vetiver grows in all types of 12-soil and in a wide range of climatic conditions. Its propagation is easy. The superior cultivar should be collected to raise the nursery. In Karnataka, six cultivars have been identified. One cultivar exhibits superior characteristics for hedge formation, fodder, insect disease, and drought resistance.

The best nursery site can be selected in loamy sands where drainage is good. Then, slips are planted in a double or e triple line to form parallel hedges in a nursery bed. The hedge rows should be 30-40 cm apart. Application of fertilizer to the slips with diammonium phosphate (DAP, @150 kg/ha Nitrogen) and irrigation once a fortnight encourages fest tillering. Dibbling of DAP into the planting furrow before planting the slips will be enough. A spade or fork is used to collect planting material to extract a vetiver clump. Then, a handful of grassroots is torn out from the clump to form the slips that are planted in the field.

The planting of slips is done at the beginning of the wet season. Holes are made 10 to 15 cm apart in the furrow that was plowed to make the contour. The slips are then pushed into each hole by taking care that the roots are not bent upwards. The slips are firmed by tightening the soil. The gaps formed by casualties should be filled by planting new slips. The plant must form a hedge.

To encourage tillering and hedge thickening, the grass should be cut back to 30-50 cm after the first year. White ant-infestation can be controlled by applying 1 kg of BHC powder for every 150 m of hedge line. Established hedges are trimmed to a height of 30-50 cm annually. Vetiver hedges take about three years to be fully effective.

The initial cost of hedge establishment is estimated at Rs. 288 per 100m of hedge. The cost to produce new hedges is relatively low, about Rs. 72 per 100m, if planting material is raised in a nursery. Hence, the economic returns are more than 100 percent. For each hectare, 250 meters of hedge is required.

Planting of Vetiver slips for hedge formation to check soil erosion.

The combined effect of contour cultivation and vetiver hedge formation do wonders even in slopy land by arresting almost total soil erosion and allowing water infiltration into sub-soil and thereby raising the ground water table in the watershed area. Some early results in alfisols and vertisols indicate that rainfall runoff was reduced from 40 percent to 15 percent (compared with the control), and silt loss was reduced from 25 tonnes per hectare to six tonnes per hectare (all for two-year-old hedges on 2 percent slopes).

Apart from preventing soil erosion, oil extracted from Vetiver's roots is very valuable and an important raw material for the perfume industry.

The roots are used for making screens (Khas Chiks), mats, handfans, baskets, etc. In dry, degraded, and exposed hilly terrain, the spongy golden root systems act as a boon to the farmers, horticulturists, and foresters in in-situ soil and moisture conservation at low cost and also in getting an additional annual income.

6. THE GLORY LILY (GARDENING, IN THE INDU)

(For Gardener, Medicinal practitioners, Cultivators)

The glory lily

You might be knowing the name of the State flower of Tamil Nadu. It is *Kannuvalipoo* (Tamil) also known as the Glory Lily which will easily draw your attention. The scarlet or crimson and yellow flowers are eye-catching during the winter months, October to January, in scrub jungles.

The botanical name is *Gloriosa superba*. A weak-stemmed ornamental herbaceous climber of a small genus *Gloriosa*, it was first observed and described by Linneaus in 1753. It belongs to the *Liliaceae* family. In India it is the only species. The other, *Gloriosa Virescens* is found in tropical South Africa, Madagascar, India to Indo-China and Malaysia.

It shoots to 4(6)m. climbing by modified leaf tip which works like a tendril. It grows commonly in low jungles almost throughout India upto a height of 1,800 metres. The 5-10 grams, but larger doses can be poisonous. The tuber is also given to cattle for the expulsion of worms. The juice prepared from leaf kills lice.

The toxic properties of the drug prepared from Gloriosa superba are due to the presence of alkaloids, chiefly colchicine ($C_{22} H_{25} O_6 N$). Colchicine is used in medicine, mainly as Salicylate, in the treatment of gout and rheumatism and in plant breeding work for inducing polyploidy.

During extensive analytical study on the various parts of the plant conducted by the Council of Scientific and Industrial Research Institute, Jammu-Tawi, it was observed that seeds are richer in colchicine than that of the tubers.

However, seeds are available in limited quantity than the tubers. Because of high content of colchicine in seeds, the cultivation

GARDENING

You might know the name of the State flower of Tamil Nadu. It is Kannuvalipoo (Tamil), also known as the Glory Lily, which will easily draw your attention. The scarlet or crimson and yellow flowers are eye-catching in scrub jungles during the winter months, from October to January.

**Kannuvalipoo (in Tamil) -the botanical name is
*Gloriosa superba.***

The botanical name is Gloriosa superba. A weak-stemmed ornamental herbaceous climber of a small genus Gloriosa, it was first observed and described by Linneaus in 1753. It belongs to the Liliaceae family. In India, it is the only species. The other, Gloriosa virescens, is found in tropical South Africa, Madagascar, India to Indo-China, and Malaysia.

It shoots to 4(6) m, climbing by a modified leaf tip, which works like a tendril. It grows commonly in low jungles almost throughout India, up to a height of 1,800 meters. The slender stems rise from a perennial, fleshy, tuberous rhizome, and the leaves are alternate, opposite. There are two varieties of this plant. The root of one divides dichotomously; that of the other does not divide at all, a single piece shooting into the ground.

The plant is known for its medicinal uses. A paste of the root is traditionally used to heal bites of poisonous insects and snakes, scorpion stings, parasitic skin diseases, and leprosy. It is said to have an effectual antidote against cobra poison when one or two pre-treated pieces of the slices of the root are given internally for cobra bite.

The tubers are regarded as tonic, stomachic, and anti-helminthic when taken in small doses, like 5-10 grams, but larger doses can be poisonous. The tuber is also given to cattle for the expulsion of worms. The juice prepared from the leaf kills lice.

The toxic properties of the drug prepared from Gloriosa superba are due to the presence of alkaloids, chiefly colchicine ($C_{22}H_{25}O_6N$). Colchicine is used in medicine, mainly as salicylate, in the treatment of gout and rheumatism, and in plant breeding work, including polyploidy.

During the extensive analytical study on the various parts of the plant conducted by the Council of Scientific and Industrial Research Institute, Jammu-Tawi, it was observed that seeds are richer in colchicine than tubers.

However, seeds are available in a limited quantity than the tubers. Because of the high content of colchicine in seeds, the cultivation of the plant has been started to a limited extent in Tamil Nadu and Karnataka.

It is propagated by divisions of rhizomes planted before the onset of monsoon in light-rich soil with good drainage. The local people used to collect the tubers by uprooting the plant indiscriminately as it fetches Rs. 15 -25 per kg. As a result, the number of naturally grown plants in the forest is fast decreasing, leading the plant to the list of endangered species. This can be discouraged by informing local people about its cultivation practices and tying up its regular marketing facility.

7. THE BEST TIMBER FOR EVERYONE FOR ALL PURPOSES

(The Science Express NATURE)

Cultivation of teak can be done even in non-forest areas under favorable conditions that include deep soil with good irrigation, sub-soil drainage facilities, and areas free from frost attack.

Teak, botanically known as Tectona grandis, is the most sought-after timber variety. The natural habitat of teak is found in two distinct regions of Southeast Asia; one covers peninsular India and the other in Burma, Thailand, and Java, where, under favorable conditions, large numbers of naturally grown seedlings can be seen in the forests.

Earlier, it was believed that teak was primarily a forest tree and could grow only in natural habitats until the world's first teak plantation was raised in the 1840s at Nilambur by H V Conolly, the then collector of Malabar, with the help of Pazhur Chattu Menon, the then sub-conservator of area.

Menon then laid a foundation for various teak plantations over the next two decades. By 1918, 6,500 acres of land in Nilambur were under teak plantation. Natural seedlings supplemented by artificial regeneration to fill up banks give better results in forest habitats. However, the cultivation of teak can be done even in non-forest areas under favorable conditions, like deep soil with good irrigation and sub-soil drainage facilities, and the area should be free from frost attacks.

Teak can be grown either by directly sowing seeds or transplanting seedlings. Both methods have largely been supplemented by the effective and efficient 'stump planting' method.

Pretreatment

Genetically superior seeds must be obtained from the forest department. Teak seed, being a hard nut, needs pre-sowing treatment to hasten germination.

Canal Bank teak in Thanjavur (24 years old)

Nursery Techniques

For growing seedlings, well-drained sandy loam or loamy soils are selected. The soil is well dug up and mixed with ash in a well-drained site. The standard size of the bed is 12m x 1.2m; it is raised in moisture localities to avoid water logging and is flat or slightly sunken in the dry zone. Pre-treated seeds (8-10 kgs) are sown in 7.5 cm x 7.5 cm lines or broadcast about 1 cm deep between February and May. Germination takes place in 10-20 days. When seedlings attain a height of 3 to 5cm, they are transplanted with the displacement of 15 X 15 cm on beds raised above the ground about 30 cm by the side support of slit bamboo/coconut leaves, or seedlings are pricked out in polythene bags (13cm x 25cm) already filled with silt, sand and farmyard manure in 1:1:1 ratio. Watering should be light every day. Entire seedlings can be planted in the field after 3-4 months.

Transplant Nursery bed

Stump Preparation

For preparation of stumps, seedlings are kept in transplant beds and watered at regular intervals. Plants are maintained in bed for 6 to 9 months. After this period, the plants develop carroty roots and are ready for stump preparation.

A trench has to be made along one side of the bed. The plants have to be pulled out with care so that the carroty taproot is not injured or broken.

Plants of normal growth and having collar diameters of not less than one cm are made into stumps. Seedlings with 10 cm girth or one to two cm diameter at the collar are the optimum size of stumps. A collar with a diameter of 1.8 cm is ideal for stumps.

The best stump material for planting is a 1 cm to 2.5 cm shoot portion and 20 cm to 23 cm root portion. Side roots are pruned and kept ready just before the planting operation.

Replanting Operations

Preliminary works like the selection of a planting site, preparation of land, alignment of pits, and providing irrigation and drainage are some of the important operations that govern the success of a teak plantation.

Selection of land is very important. A wrong selection, despite subsequent care, will be a vain attempt. All pre-planting operations should be completed before the onset of monsoon.

Planting Techniques

Stumps are planted in crow-bar holes made in refilled pits 30 cm3. A hole equal to the exact length of the stump is made in the center of the thali with an iron crow-bar about 60cm long. The stump is then inserted, and the soil is firmly pressed against it. Damp soil is necessary for successful stump planting. Stumps are buried in the soil up to the collar level. A good pre-monsoon shower makes soil compact around the stumps.

While transporting stumps, they should be kept in moist, gunny packing; while planting, the ends of the root and shoot should be freshened with a sharp, thin cut. The planting displacement generally adopted is 2m x 2m.

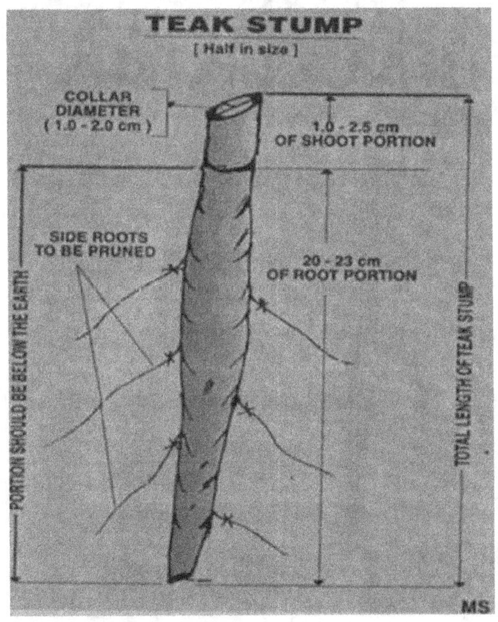

Teak Stump for planting

Plantation of stum origin

Essential points for stump planting

- The stump should be planted exactly up to the collar.

- The depth of the hole should be equal to the length of the root.

- When driving the crow-bar slant-wise and closing the hole, care must be taken so that no air spaces are left below or around the root.

- The stump must be very firmly planted.

- Every stump should be checked after planting.

Teak stumps are ideal for large-scale planting. It is economical, with a 90 percent success rate.

For medium and small-scale planting, pre-sprouted stems raised in polythene bags (16cm x 30cm), 300 gauge can be planted in 30 cm3 pits dug in advance. They can be planted in early monsoon showers and give a 100 percent survival rate. However, planting pre-sprouted stumps is costlier than stump planting.

Tending work like casualty replacement, weeding, irrigation, fertilizers, insecticides and pesticides, and thinning operations are essential for improving the crop.

Character of the Teak Tree and its distribution in India

In India, teak mainly occurs south of the Narmada and Mahanadi Rivers, Aravalli's in Rajasthan, along the Betwa and Dhasan rivers in southern Uttar Pradesh, Andhra Pradesh, Maharashtra, Tamil Nadu, Karnataka, and Kerala. It also occurred in parts of Gujarat, Bihar, and Orissa and was introduced in moist deciduous forests of West Bengal, Bihar, Assam, Orissa, and Andaman.

Controlling Factors for Teak Cultivation

Teak thrives best in a fairly moist, warm, tropical climate with an ideal annual rainfall range varying from 127 cm - 381cm, absolute maximum shade temperature varying from 35° C - 43° C, and absolute minimum from 9° C - 17° C.

The majority of the teak forests are situated on hilly or undulating land. It also grows well on the drained level of alluvial ground and alluvial pockets along rivers. It grows well in fertile and deep soils on lower slopes. Its best growth is at about 600m and below. It grows up to 1200m in the Western Ghats. Teak grows on various geological formations like the Deccan trap, crystalline rock (granite, genesis, schists), and sandstone. However, the quality depends on the depth, structure, porosity, and moisture-holding capacity of the resulting soil from the parent material and rainfall available.

Teak can be cultivated on alluvial, sandy loam, and red loamy soil except for laterite, stiff clay, and black cotton soil. Selection of the right kind of site and plating material, timely planting operations, and subsequent tending work can induce plant growth to an excellent order, making teak plantation an eco-friendly renewable national asset in addition to its viability.

8. A MEDICINAL PLANT - STRYCHNOS NUX-VOMICA

(Published in THE HINDU, GARDENING)

You might have heard of or used the common homeopathy medicine, nux vomica. It has a remedy for patients with illnesses relating to over-sensitiveness, irritable nature, mental exertion, loss of sleep, anxiety, the tendency to faint, and labor pain.

It is a medium-sized tree, botanically called Strychnos nux-vomica, belonging to the natural order of Loganiaceae. The plant was first described by Linneaus, a well-known botanist, in 1753. In Tamil, it is called Yetti or Kanjaram. The medicine, nux vomica, is prepared from the seeds, which are very bitter and contain Strychnine and Brucine. The ash-grey circular seeds remain in the fruit, which is very much like a ripe orange in color and appearance.

The plant belongs to the large genus Strychnos, comprising 200 species of trees and climbing shrubs found throughout the tropics and sub-tropics of both hemispheres. The various parts of the plant of most Strychnos species are intensely bitter, and many of these plants contain poisonous substances, especially in the bark, roots, and seed coats; some are of medicinal value. About 13 species grow in India. Of these, S. nux-vomica is the best-known species yielding the nux-vomica of commerce and renowned for the value of its alkaloids, Strychnine and Brucine. It is a middle-sized deciduous tree, attaining a girth of 1 to 1.8 m and a height of 13 m. It is usually a small crooked tree commonly found on laterite in wastelands or in degraded forests. It grows abundantly in Kankan Kanara along the Western coast. It is also found in Eastern UP, Bihar, Orissa, parts of Madhya Pradesh, Maharashtra, Andhra Pradesh, the Coromandel Coast and Karnataka.

It can be grown in a wide range of temp, i.e., 14°c to 48°c, and in wide ranges of rainfall from 900 to 3000mm or more. It grows up to a height of 1,200 m. Abundant on laterite along the sea coast in evergreen thorn scrub, it grows chiefly on deep alluvial soil.

It regenerates freely under natural conditions. For artificial regeneration, the seeds are collected from the middle of

December to the end of April. The pulp of the fruits is washed, and seeds are spread on mats in the sun to dry. The seeds can be stored for about a year in gunny bags (600-850 seeds make a kg).

For raising seedlings, seeds are dibbled in poly bag containers from March to April. It takes about a month to germinate. About 150 to 200 seedlings can be raised within a period of six months from one kg of seeds, and the seedlings can be planted during the rainy season in 30 cm x 30cm x 30cm pits for raising plantation.

The Wood is used locally, mainly for making agricultural implements. The fruits are more valuable than timber for their medicinal value.

To expand and conserve the genetic biodiversity of our country, such plants of high medicinal value must be restored in all earnest for posterity.

9. NIRMALI- A SHIELD AGAINST POLLUTION

(THE SCIENCE EXPRESS NATURE)

Nirmali trees clear dusty air, beautify the landscape and provide shade to the passers-by.

NIRMALI, commonly known as the clearing nut tree, is mentioned in Manu Samhita. In Ayurveda, Susruta mentions the use of its seeds for clearing muddy water in the chapter Water. According to the Charak Samhita, Nirmali is effective in curing eye diseases.

The thick foliage of Nirmali Seedlings has a very long tap root system

Nirmali, botanically known as *Strychnos potatorum* (Linn), belongs to the family Loganiaceae. Known as Kataka or Ambu prasada in Sanskrit, Nirmali in Hindi and Bengali, and Tettran Kottai in Tamil, it is a tall deciduous tree growing up to a height of over 12 meters. Found abundantly in West Bengal, Central India, and South India, up to an altitude of 1,200 meters, the tree is very common in dry deciduous forests of the Indian peninsula.

Its bark is thick, blackish, and corky with deep vertical cracks, and its trunk is often irregularly fluted. Leaves are elliptic, 5-12 cm long, and nearly sessile, sub coriaceous, glabrous, and shining. It has white fragrant flowers in auxiliary sessile cymes, and the fruits are berries, which are thin-shelled, deep bluish-black, and globose.

Ripe seeds are used for clearing muddy water. It settles the colloidal matter suspended in muddy water. The water-clearing quality of the seeds is due to the presence of alkaloids. Analysis of the family of powdered seeds gave the following details:

Moisture is 8.2 percent, nitrogen is 0.33 percent, alkaloids are 0.17, Brucine, ash is 1.34, and sucrose is 1-2.

Nirmali, which has dense foliage, can be grown as an ornamental tree. It is ideal for avenue plantations and suitable for plantations near building complexes, parks, and barren lands.

It acts as a shelter belt against strong winds and filters dust particles. A row of these trees at six meters of escapement will serve the purpose of clearing the dusty air, beautifying the landscape, and providing dense shade to the passers-by.

The tree is drought-hardy and has proven to withstand severe drought. Although its wood is hard in sawing, it is still suitable for making agricultural implements.

Some of the medicinal applications of Nirmali are:

In case of long-standing chronic diarrhea, which becomes resistant to other medicines, Nirmali's seed powder (about 500 milligrams) is added to a cup of water and boiled till it reduces to half the quantity.

It is then filtered and taken after meals. If it is repeated for a few days, the ailment will be cured. For people suffering from frequent attacks of cough, one gram of crushed fruit soaked in hot water for 5-7 hours gives good results. The liquid should be filtered and taken at least 3 to 4 times a day.

Belching problem: It is caused by the accumulation of fat in the abdominal region. Belching can be cured with a decoction of Nirmali's seed. Mix two grams of seeds in two cups of water and boil it till the quantity is reduced to half.

Take the decoction a couple of times with an interval of 3 to 4 hours for a few days, and the frequent belching will be cured.

A mixture of Nirmali seeds, honey, and camphor is applied to the eyes in lachrymation or copious watering from the eyes. Ripe fruits and seeds are used as antidotes against snake bites.

(Source: Chiranjeeb Banaushadhi by Ayurvedacharya Shibkali Bhattacharya)

For propagation, seeds should be collected between October and March, when berries become ripe and turn black. The seeds are extracted after removing the pulp and dried in shade. Seeds are to be pre-treated by soaking them in water for 48 hours before sowing them in the mother bed. Seeds germinate in a span of 35 to 45 days. If proper care is taken, one can get about 80 seedlings out of 100 seeds sown in the mother bed.

The seedlings have a long tap root system, which helps them withstand extreme drought.

PART III: STORIES OF SELFLESS SERVICES IN FORESTRY

10. HUGO WOOD- THE SOURCE OF MY INSPIRATION- MY HERO, IN WESTERN GHATS

HUGO WOOD (Hugo Francis Andrew Wood, 1870 - 1933)

The man who never wanted his name, fame, money, or the result of his *action* but gave him everything to bring back the lost glory of the greeneries of the Anamalai range (Anai means elephant and malai means mountain, i.e., the mountain of elephants) located in Coimbatore District of Tamil Nadu, even at his supreme sacrifice on 12.12.1933. It appears that he would not even keep any traces of his personal photograph.

In 1916, Hugo set up a bamboo hut in Mount Stuart (near Top Slip) and began working in earnest to regenerate the forest of the mountain range. He was living in that bamboo hut he constructed and began the regeneration of the Anamalai range. He never got married, cooked his own food, and lived alone.

He started small, targeting an area of 25 acres. By the time of his death, it had spread to an area of 650 sq. km. That was the result of his determination and dedication to his duty. ***The story of his sacrifice, austerity, commitment, and honesty did not stop there.***

In 1925, Hugo retired after a severe bout of tuberculosis and settled in Coonoor.

However, a few months earlier, sensing his approaching death, he sent the money needed for the tomb to be created to the chief conservator of Madras Presidency with a will he drew asking to be buried in Mount Stuart in the Western Ghats.

The inscription on the tomb reads **"Si monumentum requiris circumspice,"** Latin for **"If you are looking for my monuments, look around."**

Wood died in Coonoor on 12 December 1933 at the age of 63.

That was revered Hugo Francis Andrew Wood in brief HUGO WOOD - a British Forest Officer who served at Top Slip in the years 1916-17, stopped indiscriminate felling by the then colonial British govt, and hence we can see the lush greeneries still in Anamalai mountain.

Today, we cannot see his physical body, not even his photograph, but the living spirit of Hugo Wood remains in our hearts as the bright source of inspiration for all wisdom to move forward to protect, conserve, and augment forests in a true sense like Him...

Then Hugo Wood single-handedly converted once overharvested all important timber trees and made forest (almost barren land) into thick green cover with his innovative planting techniques when all efforts taken by his seniors like Doglus Lushington and many others failed for decades.

__I do not know whether HUGO WOOD studied the Shrimad Bhagwat Gita and followed it meticulously or not, but he was a Karm yogi and a Renunciant— means an individual who dedicated himself and completed his work as duty without expectation of any reward or result of his action as taught by Lord Krishna to Arjuna__ (in India's famous epic- the Mahabharat)

1. Hugo Wood was born to Elizabeth Maria Louisa and Thomas William Wood at Byculla in Bombay Presidency On 12 June 1870. He was their second son. Hugo Wood Scotchman studied at the Royal Indian Engineering College, Cooper's Hill, during 1890-93. He passed the Indian Public Service tests and chose forestry at the age of 23 years. He returned to India in 1893 and joined in regenerating the Ajmer forests of Rajasthan. He was dedicated to his duty and performed excellent regeneration work in Rajasthan.

2. The British Government noticed Hugo Wood's ability on regeneration work at Ajmer, and he was later sent to Godavari and Kurnool for similar work in the Madras Presidency, where he served in various capacities as Assistant Conservator of Forests and Deputy Conservator of Forests.

3. Hugo Wood came as a successor to Captain Hamilton. Douglas Lushington and Fisher failed in their attempt to regenerate the teak plantation in and around Top Slip. However, Hugo Wood believed that teak

plantations could be successfully raised at a reasonable cost using their seed source. When Wood took over as a working plan officer for the area, he advocated "concentrated artificial regeneration "of teak at 25 acres per annum after eradicating lantana (*Lantana camara* – a weed which suppresses the growth of other good plants) from the area for the period from 1919-1930. Protected measures were also prescribed. From then onward, substantial areas in Mount Surat block were brought under teak plantation till 1937.

4. The plantations he raised from 1916 to 1917 near the Mount Stuart Forest bungalow encircle the grave of the author of those plantations today. (An area of four chains long and three chains wide symmetrically round the grave of the late Hugo Wood in 1916 took plantation, below the Mount Stuart Bungalow had been demarcated as a permanent preservation plot in his honor.)

5. Wood was asked to replicate his Ajmer work in the Anamalai range in 1915. The next year, he was posted to the South Coimbatore Division (a region that included parts of present-day Tamil Nadu and Kerala) by the time the Anamalai range was left with almost no trees.

6. Wood never got married. He dedicated his life to conservation and didn't care about race, religion, ethnicity, language, or nationality. He was finally made Conservator of Forests in 1918, a post he held till 1926,

when he retired to Coonoor after suffering from tuberculosis (Tamil Nadu Forest Department booklet).

The inscription on the tomb reads *"Si monumentum requiris circumspice,"* Latin for *"If you are looking for my monuments, look around."*

A) Indiscriminate felling or extraction of teak trees in the Anamalai range in the name of scientific forestry

In the early 19th century, the colonial powers were reviving for naval supremacy. The Royal Navy needed timber for new ships to retain its supremacy. The British needed the railways for administration and trade.

Apart from this, Wood was needed for all these purposes, including fuel for steam locomotives; they needed massive amounts of teak. So, this species was needed to be grown, and other species of trees were cut down. They called it "scientific forestry".

The British continued cutting off teak trees in Anamalai. Roughly 40,000 trees were felled each year in government forests in the Madras Presidency alone for the railways. This doesn't include other species of trees that were exploited for other purposes like fuel.

The British had the Anamalai range surveyed in 1820. They decided to harvest the timber but found that they couldn't transport the trees down to the plains as they were too large. So, they came up with a novel method—they cut the trees and pushed the timber down through the slope to the river downhill. Hence, the place is called Topslip.

Due to over-exploitation, the once-green hills of Anamalai had lost much of their tree cover by 1885. For the next three decades, several British foresters tried to regenerate the region but failed.

Until 200 years ago, only tribals lived in the Anamalai range, which has the highest peak of the Western Ghats at 2,695m.

In the name of civilization, the British accomplished a few activities in a systematic manner. First, they enacted the Indian Forest Act in 1865. As per this Act, they divided the forests into three categories—reserved, protected, and village.

The Anamalai forests came under the reserved category, which meant local tribes couldn't even take twigs to use as fuel or hunt small animals for food. They banned cattle grazing. Collecting vegetables or fruits could land one in prison.

Many Adivasis, on the other hand, were forced to vacate their ancient homelands and work in British plantations for free.

To carry the huge trees, they created an elephant training camp, which exists even today. Tribals who lived in the Anamalai area of Western Ghats domesticated some elephants to become kumki elephants. They were used to drive away wild elephants to the mountain range and also carry the trees.

This went on until most of the Anamalai range was cleared up. Between 1885 and 1915, several forest officers and conservators tried to regenerate the area but were unsuccessful.

And then came Hugo Wood. This was when an officer named Hugo Wood decided to put a stop to the unchecked destruction of indigenous forests.

B) 1916 Hugo Wood joined in forestry work

He worked on regenerating the Ajmer forests of Rajasthan. His ability in this regard was noticed by the British Government, and he was later sent to Godavari and Kurnool in Madras Presidency, where he served in various capacities as assistant conservator of forests and deputy conservator of forests.

Wood was asked to replicate his Ajmer work in the Anamalai range in 1915. The next year, he was posted to the South Coimbatore Division Mount Stuart, Ulandy R.F Range, Top Slip, the Anamalai range in the Western Ghats

C) Hugo Wood's Contribution to Forestry and Conservation

He understood the importance of the Western Ghats to the Indian climate, as well as the dangers of deforestation and the importance of conservation. In 1915, Wood drew up a working plan for regenerating the forests of the Western Ghats, especially in Anamalai and the surrounding areas.

Second, he admonished the British for uprooting trees and introduced coppicing. This is a method of forest management that takes advantage of the fact that many trees will rapidly regrow in the spring if they are cut down up to the stump during the winter. It is friendly to wildlife and other flora and fauna.

Third, Wood befriended the tribals, and many who were displaced were brought back. He restored the customary rights of those who lived near the forests in the Anamalai range.

Finally, he marked out areas where no felling or coppicing was allowed for 25 years. The British Government agreed to this plan as they had unsuccessfully tried regenerating the Anamalai range for 30 years. **Wood** also refused to provide to the British during World War I.

In 1916, Wood, living in a bamboo hut in Mount Stuart, began the regeneration of the Anamalai range.

First, he analyzed why the teak trees were not growing back and discovered that it was due to the presence of *Lantana camara*, a flowering shrub that is actually a weed; Wood made sure to get rid of it all.

Despite the fear of cholera and malaria due to the climate in the region, he worked in earnest. He would go on daily walks into the deforested land 4km away, pockets filled with teak seeds.

He lived alone, cooked his own food, and never missed out on a daily ritual. During his daily walks in the deforested land, he would fish out fistfuls of teak seeds from his pockets, use his silver-tipped walking stick to poke a hole in the ground, and plant seeds there. He did this at 15 ft intervals.

He would repeat the process till his pockets were empty. Then, he would go back for more seeds and start again from where he left off. He also made efforts to rid the hills of *Lantana camara,* an invasive species of flowering shrub that hampered the growth of teak.

Appointed the District Forest Officer of Coimbatore South Division in September 1915 (a post he would hold till 1926), Hugo decided to put a stop to the unchecked destruction of Anamalai's forests and drew up a working plan for the same.

First, the 45-year-old Scotsman talked to the local colonial authorities and convinced them to stop hunting wildlife and the irresponsible chopping of trees. He also befriended the tribals who lived near the forests, restored their traditional rights, and brought back many who had been displaced (due to the British bringing the Anamalai forests under the reserved category).

Next, Hugo scathingly admonished the British Government for uprooting trees and introduced the forest management technique of coppicing — a method that takes advantage of the fact that many trees rapidly regrow during spring if they are cut down up to the stump during the winter.

Finally, he marked out areas where no logging or coppicing would be allowed for a period of 25 years. In fact, such was his dedication to his work that he refused to provide timber to the British during World War I (1914-1918).

In 1916, Hugo set up a bamboo hut in Mount Stuart (near Topslip) and began working in earnest to regenerate the forest of the mountain range. He started small, targeting an area of 25 acres. By the time of his death, it had spread to an area of 650 sq. km.

Hugo's hard work paid off, breathing new life into the hills of Anamalai.

D) Hugo Wood's Death and Legacy

He dedicated his life to conservation and didn't care about race, religion, ethnicity, language, or nationality. He was finally made conservator of forests in 1918, a post he held till 1925.

In 1925, Hugo retired after a severe bout of tuberculosis and settled in Coonoor, according to a Tamil Nadu Forest Department booklet. Wood died in Coonoor on 12 December at the age of 63.

However, a few months earlier, sensing his approaching death, he drew a will asking to be buried in Mount Stuart in the Western Ghats and also sent the money needed for the tomb to the chief conservator of Madras Presidency.

On 13 December 1933, the first motor vehicle that drove up Anamalai's mountainous road to Topslip was a small lorry carrying the body of Hugo Wood. It was followed by 11 cars with British officials.

He now lies buried among the teak trees and his legacy. The inscription on the tomb reads **"Si monumentum requiris circumspice," Latin for "If you are looking for my monuments, look around."**

On his death, this request was conceded, and Hugo Wood was laid to rest among his lasting legacy — the teak trees he had raised in the hills of Anamalai.

On windy days, leaves gently float down from the trees onto the tombstone as if to pay homage to the man who so completely loved the Anaimalais and who did so much to save it.

HALL OF FAME
H.F.A. WOOD

Mr. Hugo Francis Andrew Wood after joining the Imperial Forest Service in 1890, received his professional training at Royal Indian Engineering College at Cooper's Hill, came to India during 1893 and worked in Madras Presidency up to his retirement in 1926. He worked in various capacities, as Assistant Conservator of Forests, Deputy Conservator of Forests and rose to the rank of Conservator of Forests in 1918 and retired in 1926.

He is remembered for his work in the Godavari, Kurnool and South Coimbatore Forsest Divisions. Despite his ill health on account of malaria ridden forests, he worked without a break for almost ten years. He prevented serious forest fires by practicing early burning of grass.

He tackled the unruly aborigine Chenchu who, with their bow and arrow had intimidated everyone, pursuing the easy way of timber thieving, robbery and blackmail. Wood tackled the problem by providing them labour in teak plantations, by instituting provision stores and civilizing influences of all kinds. He had such a great influence over the people that even after he had left the district, they revered his presence.

He was unrivalled as the mentor of the young officers and their later achievements bear ample testimony to his qualities. He was modest and very kind to the people around him.

He is renowned for his work at the Anamalai Hills of Coimbatore. As the teak of the area provided supplies to the construction of ships of the Royal Navy, regenerating the trees became a major task which he faced boldly in spite of the difficulties due to lack of water, labour and malaria. He formulated a working plan of his own for raising teak plantations and was a truly 'a hands on' professional.

During 1916-17, he experimented near his Mount Stuart residence and in the Ulandy valley and proved that teak plantations could be raised successfully from seed source at a reasonable cost. He was the Working Plan Officer and advocated 'concentrated artificial regeneration' method of teak and substantial areas were brought under teak plantations till 1937. This, he accomplished by living not in the comfort of a forest bungalow, but in a bamboo hut on the edge of his plantation.

A sportsman in the true sense of the word, he was as kind and generous to the wild animals as to his fellow man.

Retiring to Ootacamund, Wood devoted himself to gardening and fishing in which he was exceedingly successful.

Mr. Wood died in Ootacamund on 12.12.1933 at the age of 63. At his own request, Wood was laid to rest among the plantations he created at Anamalais.

His interest in the work of the department was dedicated and unflagging. The early teak plantations raised by him near the Mount Stuart forest bungalow encircle his grave even today. This area has been demarcated as a permanent preservation plot in his honour, a living memorial to him. The monument is one of the unique sites so much so, each of the training batch of Forest Guards, Foresters, Rangers, SFS and IFS Probationers never miss the opportunity to visit this legendary spot.

The inscriptions on the grave is very simple reads as "SI MONUMENTUM REQUIRS CIRCUMSPICE" meaning, " If you want to see me, look around" Such is the inspiring message left by Hugo Wood for the next generations. *

***(This article is composed by compiling various published References as mentioned below**

1. The HINDU, The Hall of Fame - Tamil Nadu Forest Department 2016, The Times of India, The Nakkeeran Tamil Weekly

2. DEEPA KANDASAMY

3.Sanchari Pal and 4. Google Search)

11. SAALUMARADA THIMMAKKA, AN ENVIRONMENTALIST FROM KARNATAKA

Saalumarada Thimmakka's story serves as an inspiration for environmentalists and individuals worldwide, emphasizing the significance of taking initiative at the local level to contribute to the well-being of the planet.

Saalumarada Thimmakka, whose full name is Saalumarada Thimmakka Gowda, is an Indian environmentalist hailing from Karnataka, India. Born in 1910 in Hulikal village in Karnataka, she gained widespread recognition for her extraordinary efforts in environmental conservation.

Thimmakka was born in Hulikal village, and just like any other woman in her village, she worked as a laborer and did not get any formal education. She was married off to a cattle herder named Bekal Chikkayya, but the couple could not conceive even after 25 years of marriage.

Instead of cursing their fate, the couple tried to fill the void by planting and tending banyan trees as their own children. Every day, they would carry buckets of water and travel four kilometers to water the banyan saplings.

She, unfortunately, lost her husband in 1991, but the tragedy could not deviate her from her selfless work.

One of her most remarkable achievements is the planting of over 8000 trees, including banyan trees, along a 4-kilometer stretch of highway between Hulikal and Kudur. She, along with her husband, began this initiative in the 1950s, and over the years, the couple nurtured these trees like their own children. The famous tree-lined avenue is often referred to as the "Saalumarada Thimmakka Road" in her honor.

Saalumarada Thimmakka's work is a testament to her commitment to the environment and her desire to make a positive impact on the world. Despite facing various challenges and hardships, she continued her tree-planting mission with determination.

In recognition of her incredible efforts, Thimmakka has received numerous awards and honors. Her inclusion in the BBC's list of the most influential and inspirational women is a testament to the global recognition of her work. This recognition also highlights the importance of grassroots efforts in environmental conservation and the impact that individuals can have on a larger scale.

Saalumarada Thimmakka's story serves as an inspiration for environmentalists and individuals worldwide, emphasizing the significance of taking initiative at the local level to contribute to the well-being of the planet.

Saalumarada Thimmakka, an environmentalist from Karnataka, has been listed among BBC's most influential & inspirational 100 women. She is the oldest person on the list for planting more than 8000 trees in 80 years.

She lives an ordinary life, but she is no ordinary woman. In her own village, she got the honor of being named 'Saalumarada' for the work she has been doing for eight decades. The word 'Saalumarada' means 'row of trees' in the Kannada language. She planted and nurtured 384 banyan trees lined in a five-km stretch some 80km from Bangalore.

Awards and Work Saalumarada Thimmakka and her great afforestation project remained unknown until she received the National Citizens Award in 1996. For her achievements, she was conferred with many prestigious awards, such as the Nadoja Award, Karnataka Kalpavalli Award, Godfrey Phillip Award, and Vishwathama Award. Thimmakka's Resources for Environmental Education, an environmental organization based in the US, is named after her.

Thimmakka has also played an important role in constructing a water tank to store rainwater in her village. She also dreams of constructing a hospital.

**(This article is compiled from following references

1.   Google search

2.   ChatGPT

"The Forest is a peculiar organism of unlimited kindness and benevolence that makes no demands for its sustenance and extends generously the products of its life and activity; it affords protection to all beings."

- Buddhist Sutra

DISCLAIMER

This book is intended solely for informational purposes, aiming to shed light on the vital role the Kingdom of plants plays in sustaining life. The information presented herein, from the microscopic mosses to the towering trees, is offered as a means to enhance awareness and appreciation for the fundamental services plants provide—accounting for 80% of our daily sustenance and 98% of the oxygen we breathe.

The narratives within delve into the Plant kingdom's role as a repository for the Basic Life Supporting System (BLISS!), encompassing food, air, water, fertile soil, life-saving drugs, and the silent wisdom communicated akin to monks. The inclusion of the inspiring story of Hugo Wood, an IFS Officer in India, serves to inspire action towards the protection, conservation, and nurturing of our forests—the very roots of our survival.

This book is not a substitute for professional advice, and the author assumes no responsibility for any consequences resulting from the information presented. Readers are encouraged to seek professional guidance for specific situations and to act responsibly in their interactions with the botanical world. Your engagement with this book signifies your understanding of its informational nature and the importance of fostering a deeper connection with the plant kingdom.

ABOUT THE AUTHORS

Both Dr Manoj Sarkar and Dr Aruna Basu are from the Indian Forest Service (retd.) and did their doctorate in Botany. They put in about 30 years of service as senior-level officers. Their cadre was allotted to Tamil Nadu.

They love Forests and plants. Both of them are prolific writers on plants in scientific journals and als0 in daily newspapers. Their books on botany, medicinal plants are published by the Tamil Nadu Govt and also by the Govt of India. The present book is part of a series on the author-niche 'Self-Mastery through the Kingdom of Plants' to create awareness, love, and care to protect the plant community and protect ourselves.

75th **Republic Day,** (26 th January, 2024)

'TAISHA', Chennai - 600 092, INDIA

MAY WE ASK YOU A FAVOR?

At the outset, we want to give you a big thanks for reading this book. You could have chosen any other book, but you took ours, and we appreciate this. We hope you have at least a few actionable insights that will positively impact your daily life.

Can we ask for 30 seconds more of your time?

We'd love it if you could leave a review of the book. That will help us grow our readership by encouraging folks to take a chance on our books.

Keeping it straight - *reviews are the lifeblood of any author.*

It will take less than a minute of your time but will tremendously help us reach out to more people. **Kindly provide your review at the store you bought this book from.** And we'd love to see your review. Thanks for your support.